Table of Contents

Introduction

Reducing the carbs in your diet is a fantastic way to up your energy and even drop those excess pounds, both of which will leave you feeling and looking phenomenal all day. However, one of the challenges many people face while sticking to a low-carb eating plan is the meal planning required. You can't simply slap something between two pieces of bread and go. No, eating low-carb means thinking about the combination of things you are putting in your body. You actually have to prep, chop, and prepare if you are determined to obtain that slim, sexy body you've always wanted.

And it doesn't matter if you've had a long day and are feeling about as energetic as a snail. You need to eat, and that's when people go astray, either ordering carb- and preservative-dripping take-out or whipping up something quick and easy like pasta or a sandwich.

We are pleased to share with you a third option that's going to help you eat delicious low-carb meals without any fuss. Welcome to your Low-Carb Dump Meals cookbook, which includes meals you can dump into a single pot, dish, or bowl and then forget about it while you take a load off.

The key to low-carb eating is limiting your sugars and carbohydrates so your body goes into a ketogenic state, which means it burns up the fat stocks in your body like nobody's business. In order to get your body into that ketogenic state, you need to stop eating simple carbohydrates and replace them with lots of veggies and proteins like meats and nuts.

Processed foods should be avoided since they contain all sorts of hidden dangers including high levels of sugars and carbs. Dairy products can be enjoyed but should make up a smaller portion of your diet than veggies and meats.

The recipes we've created stay true to the low-carb eating concept with delicious meals like Lime Zing Fajitas, Chicken and Sweet Potato Bake, and Mint Pork Chops. We've even included a healthy vegetarian section for low-carb eating with recipes like Cauliflower Coconut Curry and Slow-Cooked Green Eggs for a morning boost that will have you rocketing all day long.

Dump meals in this cookbook are prepared in 30 minutes or less in 3 easy steps:

1. Prepare, often ahead of time, your ingredients,
2. Literally dump them in one pot, be it a slow cooker, Dutch oven, stir-frying pan, bowl, ect.
3. And then, all you need to do, is let your dump meal cook and you are done!

Cooking can definitely feel like a daunting task when you'd rather relax, but it doesn't have to be difficult. You don't need to prep and fluff like your favorite TV chefs do. In fact, you don't even have to use more than one pot when you're creating delicious dump meals. So get back to low-carb! Welcome to life getting a whole lot easier!

Bon appétit!

Chicken Recipes

Chicken Tikka Masala and Cauliflower Rice Casserole

Serves: 4
Preparation time: 10 minutes
Cooking Time: 35 minutes

Ingredients

1 lb boneless skinless chicken breasts
1 onion, chopped
1 medium cauliflower
2 cups plum tomatoes, chopped
2 cups low-sodium chicken broth
1 cup coconut milk
4 cloves garlic, minced
1 tsp ginger
1 tsp curry powder
1 tsp salt
1 tsp black pepper
½ tsp cumin seeds
Olive oil

Directions

1. Pre-heat the oven to 400°F /204°C
2. Grate cauliflower into rice-like consistency. You can use a food processor or a grate.
3. Slice chicken breasts into 1" cubes.
4. Heat 3 tbsp olive oil in cast iron skillet on medium-high heat.
5. Add cumin seeds and toast for 30 seconds.
6. Add onions, garlic, ginger, and sauté for 30 seconds.
7. Add chicken breasts, and cook until browned.
8. Mix in remaining ingredients, and sprinkle cauliflower rice on top.
9. Cover and place in the oven for 35-40 minutes, or until the chicken is cooked through and juices run clear when poked with a fork.

Nutrition (g)

Calories 434
Fat 25
Sodium 827 (mg)
Carbs 13
Sugar 7
Protein 41

Spicy Peanut Chicken

Serves: 4
Preparation time: 10 minutes
Cooking Time: 8 hours

Ingredients
1 lb boneless skinless chicken breasts
½ cup organic peanut butter
3 tbsp soy sauce
1 cup filtered water
1 tsp salt
2 tsp red chili pepper flakes
Olive oil

Directions

1. Lightly coat a slow cooker with olive oil.
2. Slice chicken breasts 1" chunks.
3. Place ingredients in slow cooker and cook on low for 8 hours.

Nutrition (g)
Calories 412
Fat 25
Sodium 1504 (mg)
Carbs 7
Sugar 3
Protein 42

Pepper Fiesta Chicken

Serves: 4
Preparation time: 10 minutes
Cooking Time: 8 hours

Ingredients

1 lb boneless skinless chicken breasts
1 large white onion, sliced
2 red bell peppers, seeded and julienned
2 green bell peppers, seeded and julienned
1 yellow bell peppers, seeded and julienned
2 jalapeño peppers, seeded and sliced
4 cloves garlic, minced
1 cup medium cheddar cheese, shredded
1 tsp oregano
1 tsp paprika
1 tsp cumin
1 tsp salt
1 tsp black pepper
2 tbsp olive oil

Directions

1. Place all ingredients but the cheddar cheese in slow cooker.
2. Cook on low for 8 hours.
3. In the last ½ hour of cooking, sprinkle with cheddar cheese.

Nutrition (g)

Calories 456
Fat 25
Sodium 862 (mg)
Carbs 14
Sugar 8
Protein 42

Rosemary Chicken with Zucchini Noodles

Serves: 4
Preparation time: 10 minutes
Cooking Time: 20 minutes

Ingredients

1 lb boneless skinless chicken breasts
4 zucchinis, peeled
1 red bell pepper, sliced
1 onion, chopped
1 tsp rosemary
1 tsp salt
1 tsp black pepper
Coconut oil

Directions

1. Preheat oven to 450°F/232°C. Place oven rack in the middle position. Coat a casserole dish with coconut oil.
2. Using a vegetable peeler, create long noodles out of zucchini.
3. Slice chicken breasts into ½" wide strips.
4. Combine ingredients in casserole dish, drizzle with 3 tbsp of melted coconut oil. Cook in oven for 20-30 minutes or until the chicken is cooked through and juices run clear when poked with a fork.

Nutrition (g)

Calories 328
Fat 16
Sodium 701 (mg)
Carbs 12
Sugar 6
Protein 36

Cheesy Chicken and Sweet Potato Bake

Serves: 4
Preparation time: 10 minutes
Cooking Time: 45 minutes

Ingredients
8 boneless skinless chicken thighs
2 sweet potatoes, peeled
1 cup mozzarella cheese
1 tsp salt
1 tsp black pepper
1 tsp dry oregano
Olive oil

Directions

1. Preheat oven to 350°F/177°C and coat a casserole dish with a little olive oil.
2. Slice sweet potatoes into ½" thick discs.
3. Place discs on bottom of pan, sprinkle with half the salt, black pepper, and oregano.
4. Top sweet potato with chicken thighs, sprinkle with remaining spices.
5. Top with mozzarella, cover with aluminum foil, and bake in oven for 45-50 minutes or until the chicken is thoroughly cooked and juices run clear when poked with a fork.

Nutrition (g)
Calories 510
Fat 20
Sodium 838 (mg)
Carbs 23
Sugar 0
Protein 59

California Chicken

Serves: 4
Preparation time: 10 minutes
Cooking Time: 30 minutes

Ingredients
1 lb boneless skinless chicken breasts
2 navel oranges
½ cup unsweetened orange juice
2 green onions, chopped
1 avocado, pitted and sliced
2 green onions, chopped
4 cloves garlic, minced
1 tsp salt
1 tsp black pepper
Olive oil

Directions

1. Preheat the oven to 400°F/204°C.
2. Heat 2 tbsp olive oil in Dutch oven over medium heat.
3. Add garlic and chicken breasts, brown for 3-4 minutes. Remove from heat.
4. Add remaining ingredients and stir a few times.
5. Cover and bake in the oven 35 minutes.

Nutrition (g)
Calories 443
Fat 25
Sodium 684 (mg)
Carbs 18
Sugar 11
Protein 34

Chunky Chicken Soup

Serves: 4
Preparation time: 5 minutes
Cooking Time: 8 hours

Ingredients
3/4 lb boneless chicken breasts
2 green apples, peeled, cored, and sliced
2 carrots, chopped
2 celery stalks, chopped
1 sweet potato, peeled and chopped
1 medium onion, chopped
4 cups low-sodium chicken broth
1 tsp rosemary
1 tsp salt
1 tsp black pepper
2 tbsp olive oil

Directions

1. Slice chicken breasts into ½" cubes.
2. Combine all ingredients in a slow cooker, mix.
3. Cook on low for 8 hours.

Nutrition (g)
Calories 260
Fat 11
Sodium 526 (mg)
Carbs 17
Sugar 9
Protein 24

Cheesy Broccoli Chicken

Serves: 4
Preparation time: 10 minutes
Cooking Time: 35 minutes

Ingredients
8 boneless skinless chicken thighs
8 cups broccoli florets
1 medium onion, diced
½ cup cheddar cheese, shredded
1 tsp black pepper
1 tsp salt
¼ cup olive oil

Directions

1. Preheat oven to 400°F/204°C and lightly coat casserole dish with a little olive oil.
2. Place all ingredients except the cheese in a large freezer bag, shake to mix.
3. Dump everything into the casserole dish, sprinkle with cheese and bake for 35 minutes or until the chicken is cooked through and juices run clear when poked with a fork.

Nutrition (g)
Calories 616
Fat 32
Sodium 901 (mg)
Carbs 15
Sugar 4
Protein 66

Sesame Sweet Ginger Chicken Wings

Serves: 4
Preparation time: 10 minutes
Cooking Time: 7 hours

Ingredients

1 lb chicken wings
¼ cup liquid honey
2 lemons, juiced
1 tbsp fresh ginger, grated
¼ cup sesame seeds
2 cups low-sodium chicken broth
1 tsp salt

Directions

1. Combine honey, ginger, lemon, sesame seeds, chicken broth, and salt in a bowl.
2. Place wings in slow cooker, pour sauce over the wings.
3. Cook on high for 7 hours.

Nutrition (g)

Calories 352
Fat 13
Sodium 717 (mg)
Carbs 24
Sugar 18
Protein 36

Cracked Pepper Chicken Wings and Sweet Potato Fries

Serves: 6
Preparation time: 10 minutes
Cooking Time: 35 minutes

Ingredients
3 lbs chicken wings
2 sweet potatoes
2 lemons, juiced
2 tbsp cracked black pepper
2 tbsp salt
Olive oil

Directions

1. Preheat oven to 400°F/204C and coat roasting tray with olive oil.
2. Combine lemon juice, cracked black pepper, salt, and 4 tbsp olive oil in bowl, add chicken wings, and toss to coat.
3. Slice sweet potatoes into thick-cut fries, place in dish with chicken wings, mix.
4. Dump the whole thing into roasting tray, arrange items in single layer.
5. Cook for 35 minutes, turning halfway through.

Nutrition (g)
Calories 752
Fat 13
Sodium 717 (mg)
Carbs 24
Sugar 18
Protein 36

Middle Eastern Tahini Molasses Chicken

Serves: 4
Preparation time: 10 minutes
Cooking Time: 35 minutes

Ingredients

8 boneless skinless chicken thighs
¼ cup tahini
¼ cup molasses, preferably grape
½ tsp red pepper flakes
¼ cup olive oil
½ tsp sea salt

Directions

1. Combine tahini, molasses, red pepper flakes, and olive oil in bowl, mix well.
2. Add chicken, marinate for 30 minutes.
3. Preheat oven to 375°F/191°C, coat casserole dish with a little olive oil.
4. Place thighs in a baking dish, cover with aluminum foil, and cook in the oven for 35-40 minutes.

Nutrition (g)

Calories 537
Fat 29
Sodium 339 (mg)
Carbs 19
Sugar 12
Protein 53

Beef Recipes

Dripping Delicious Roast

Serves: 6-8
Preparation time: 10 minutes
Cooking Time: 8 hours

Ingredients
3 lb chuck roast
2 carrots, chopped
1 large onion, chopped
2 stalks celery, chopped
4 cloves garlic, chopped
Salt
Black pepper
Olive oil

Directions

1. Coat the bottom and sides of a large slow cooker with oil.
2. Place onion, carrot, celery, and garlic in bottom of slow cooker.
3. Generously salt and pepper the pot roast and place on top of veggies.
4. Cook on low for 8 hours.

Nutrition (g)
Calories 457
Fat 18
Sodium 479 (mg)
Carbs 4
Sugar 2
Protein 65

Billy's Chili

Serves: 4
Preparation time: 10 minutes
Cooking Time: 45 minutes

Ingredients

1 lb lean ground beef
1 medium onion, chopped
2 carrots, finely chopped
2 stalks celery, finely chopped
4 cloves garlic, minced
4 cups organic tomato sauce
1 tsp oregano
1 tsp cumin
½ tsp paprika
1 tsp salt
Olive oil

Directions

1. Add 1 tbsp olive oil in a Dutch oven. Brown beef until cooked through, about 4-6 minutes on medium heat.
2. Drain excess grease.
3. Stir in remaining ingredients, cover and cook on low for 45 minutes.

Nutrition (g)

Calories 335
Fat 12
Sodium 1953 (mg)
Carbs 19
Sugar 12
Protein 38

Lime Zing Fajitas

Serves: 4
Preparation time: 10 minutes
Cooking Time: 5 minutes

Ingredients
1 lb rib eye steak
2 red bell peppers, seeded and julienned
1 red onion, peeled and sliced
16 leaves Boston lettuce
2 limes, juiced
1 tsp black pepper
1 tsp Himalayan pink salt
Olive oil

Directions

1. Slice steak against the grain.
2. Heat 4 tbsp olive oil in cast iron skillet.
3. Add steak, onion, bell peppers, salt, and black pepper, sauté for 5 minutes.
4. Add lime juice, remove from heat, and rest for 10 minutes.
5. Scoop into Boston lettuce leaves, wrap and serve.

Nutrition (g)
Calories 314
Fat 16
Sodium 1418 (mg)
Carbs 11
Sugar 4
Protein 32

Thai Beef Curry

Serves: 6
Preparation time: 5 minutes
Cooking Time: 25 minutes

Ingredients
1 lb chuck steak
2 red bell peppers, seeded and julienned
1 ½ cup green beans
1 medium onion, sliced
1 tbsp ginger, grated
1 can coconut milk
1 tbsp lemongrass, chopped
1 tsp salt
1 tsp black pepper
1 tsp curry powder
Olive oil

Directions

1. Slice steak against grain into ½" wide strips.
2. Heat 3 tbsp olive oil in large cast iron skillet over medium-high heat. Add steak, onion, and bell pepper, and sauté for 2 minutes.
3. Reduce heat to medium. Add remaining ingredients, cover and cook for 25 minutes. Stir a few times during the cooking process.

Nutrition (g)
Calories 547
Fat 42
Sodium 465 (mg)
Carbs 19
Sugar 8
Protein 28

Mango Beef Tenderloin

Serves: 6
Preparation time: 10 minutes
Cooking Time: 30 minutes

Ingredients
1 lb beef tenderloin
1½ cups fresh or frozen mango
2 red bell peppers, seeded and diced
1 large red onion, chopped in large chunks
½ cup fresh mint, chopped
1 tsp salt
1 tsp black pepper
½ tsp red chili flakes
Olive oil

Directions

1. Preheat oven to 385°F/196°F.
2. Rub tenderloin with salt, black pepper.
3. Combine 3 tbsp olive oil, mango, bell pepper, red onion, mint, and red chili flakes in casserole dish, and place tenderloin on top. Tent with foil.
4. Cook in oven for 40 minutes.

Nutrition (g)
Calories 547
Fat 42
Sodium 465 (mg)
Carbs 19
Sugar 8
Protein 28

Steak and Green Bean Stir Fry

Serves: 4
Preparation time: 5 minutes
Cooking Time: 15 minutes

Ingredients

1 lb chuck steak
3 cups green beans
2 carrots, sliced
1 medium onion, sliced
½ tsp rosemary
1 tsp salt
1 tsp black pepper
Olive Oil

Directions

1. Slice steak against the grain into ½" strips.
2. Heat 4 tbsp olive oil in skillet.
3. Add all ingredients, save spices.
4. Stir-fry 3-4 minutes.
5. Add spices, cover and cook on low for 10 minutes.

Nutrition (g)

Calories 396
Fat 22
Sodium 689 (mg)
Carbs 12
Sugar 4
Protein 37

Cheesy Beef and Brussels Sprouts Bake

Serves: 4
Preparation time: 10 minutes
Cooking Time: 30 minutes

Ingredients

1 lb sirloin steak

15 Brussels sprouts, quartered

1 tsp garlic powder

2 cups diced tomatoes

1 cup mozzarella cheese, shredded

1 tsp salt

1 tsp black pepper

Olive oil

Directions

1. Preheat oven to 400°F/204°C and coat a casserole dish with olive oil.
2. Slice steak into 1" cubes and season with salt, black pepper and garlic powder.
3. Place Brussels sprouts on bottom of dish, top with steak, tomatoes and cheese.
4. Cover and bake in oven for 45 minutes.

Nutrition (g)

Calories 386

Fat 16

Sodium 828 (mg)

Carbs 13

Sugar 4

Protein 47

Delicious Deconstructed Zucchini Lasagna

Serves: 4
Preparation time: 10 minutes
Cooking Time: 30 minutes

Ingredients

6 zucchinis, peeled
1 ½ lbs lean ground beef
1 red onion, sliced
4 cloves garlic, minced
1 cup organic tomato sauce
1 cup mozzarella cheese
1 tsp salt
1 tsp black pepper
1 tsp oregano
Olive oil

Directions

1. Preheat oven at 385°F/196°C.
2. Slice zucchini lengthwise into ½" thick strips
3. Brown beef in Dutch oven, mix in salt and black pepper.
4. Pat the beef down, sprinkle with onions and garlic.
5. Next place zucchini strips on top.
6. Top with tomato sauce and sprinkle the cheese on top.
7. Cover and place Dutch oven in oven for 30 minutes.
8. Remove cover and broil cheese topping for 1-3 minutes until golden brown.

Nutrition (g)

Calories 318
Fat 11
Sodium 833 (mg)
Carbs 12
Sugar 6
Protein 43

Philly Cheese Steak

Serves: 2
Preparation time: 10 minutes
Cooking Time: 45 minutes

Ingredients
1 lb sirloin steak
1 cup mozzarella cheese, shredded
2 cups mushrooms, sliced
2 green bell peppers, seeded and sliced
1 large onion, sliced
1 tsp black pepper
1 tsp salt
Olive oil

Directions

1. Preheat oven to 400°F/204°C.
2. Slice steak against grain into ½" wide strips.
3. Heat 4 tbsp olive oil in skillet.
4. Dump steak and veggies into skillet, stir-fry for two minutes, top with cheese and into the oven for 10 minutes.

Nutrition (g)
Calories 393
Fat 19
Sodium 832 (mg)
Carbs 10
Sugar 4
Protein 45

Beef and Broccoli Sauté

Serves: 4
Preparation time: 10 minutes
Cooking Time: 20 minutes

Ingredients
1 lb chuck steak
5 cups broccoli florets
1 onion, chopped
4 cloves garlic, minced
¼ cup coconut aminos or low sodium soya sauce
1 tsp black pepper
1 tsp paprika
Olive oil

Directions

1. Slice steak into ½" wide strips.
2. Heat olive oil in skillet.
3. Add remaining ingredients, sauté for 5 minutes.
4. Cover and cook for 20 minutes

Nutrition (g)
Calories 387
Fat 19
Sodium 137 (mg)
Carbs 15
Sugar 3
Protein 39

Beef and Spinach Bake

Serves: 4
Preparation time: 10 minutes
Cooking Time: 40 minutes

Ingredients
20 oz beef tenderloin
10 cups spinach, chopped
1 onion, diced
4 cloves garlic, minced
1 tbsp tomato paste
1 tsp salt
Olive oil

Directions

1. Preheat oven to 375°F/191°C and coat a casserole dish with olive oil.
2. Slice beef tenderloin against the grain into ½" wide strips.
3. Place tenderloin in casserole dish, mix in tomato paste.
4. Top with remaining ingredients and 4 tbsp extra virgin olive oil.

Bake in oven for 40-45 minutes, covering halfway through.

Nutrition (g)
Calories 292
Fat 24
Sodium 730 (mg)
Carbs 7
Sugar 2
Protein 44

Pork Recipes

Ginger Pork and Veggies

Serves: 4
Preparation time: 10 minutes
Cooking Time: 8 hours

Ingredients
1 lb pork tenderloin
8 cups spring vegetables mix
1 tbsp fresh ginger, grated
¼ cup reduced-sodium soya sauce
1 tsp black pepper
Coconut oil

Directions

1. Slice pork tenderloin into ½" wide strips.
2. Coat a slow cooker with coconut oil.
3. Place pork on bottom.
4. Top with vegetables, ginger, soy sauce, and black pepper. Cook on low for 8 hours.

Nutrition (g)
Calories 359
Fat 11
Sodium 964 (mg)
Carbs 3
Sugar 0
Protein 35

Pork and Apple Bake

Serves: 2
Preparation time: 10 min.
Cooking Time: 40 minutes

Ingredients
4 boneless pork chops
2 McIntosh apples, peeled and cored
1 onion, sliced
1 tsp salt
1 tsp black pepper
1 tsp rosemary
1 cup low-sodium chicken stock
Olive oil

Directions

1. Preheat oven to 385°F/196C, lightly coat a casserole dish with olive oil.
2. Rub pork chops with spices and place in casserole dish.
3. Add onion, apples, and chicken stock, and bake in oven for 40 minutes, turning halfway.

Nutrition (g)
Calories 253
Fat 8
Sodium 682 (mg)
Carbs 16
Sugar 11
Protein 31

Bacon and Eggs and Tomato

Serves: 2
Preparation time: 5 minutes
Cooking Time: 7 hours

Ingredients
4 eggs
2 tomatoes, halved
8 slices bacon
Salt
Black pepper
Olive oil

Directions

1. Coat bottom of slow cooker with olive oil.
2. Place tomatoes in bottom of slow cooker.
3. Crack eggs on top, sprinkle with salt and black pepper
4. Top with bacon slices.
5. Cook on low for 7 hours.

Nutrition (g)
Calories 211
Fat 17
Sodium 433 (mg)
Carbs 3
Sugar 2
Protein 11

Parmesan Pancetta Chicken Casserole

Serves: 2
Preparation time: 10 minutes
Cooking Time: 35 minutes

Ingredients

½ lb pancetta ham, diced
1 large chicken breast, about 12 oz, cubed
2 cups tomatoes, diced
2 green bell peppers, seeded and diced
½ cup parmesan cheese
1 medium onion, sliced
½ tsp oregano
½ tsp salt
4 tbsp olive oil (plus some for coating)

Directions

1. Preheat oven to 400°F/204°C and coat casserole with olive oil.
2. Dump ingredients into a casserole dish.
3. Tent with foil and bake for 35 minutes.

Nutrition (g)

Calories 705
Fat 47
Sodium 1198 (mg)
Carbs 12
Sugar 6
Protein 60

Mint Pork Chops

Serves: 4
Preparation time: 10 minutes
Cooking Time: 45 minutes

Ingredients

4 boneless pork chops
1 cup mint leaves
Salt
Black pepper
Extra virgin olive oil

Directions

1. Preheat oven 375°F/191F and lightly coat a casserole dish with oil.
2. Place mint, 5 tbsp olive oil, salt, and black pepper in blender and mix.
3. Dump mint sauce and pork chops in bowl, coat pork chops well.
4. Place chops in casserole dish and bake for 45 minutes.

Nutrition (g)

Calories 280
Fat 17
Sodium 110 (mg)
Carbs 2
Sugar 0
Protein 30

Fish and Seafood Recipes

Lemon Shrimp Stir-Fry

Serves: 2
Preparation time: 5 minutes
Cooking Time: 7 minutes

Ingredients

1 lb shrimp, shelled and deveined
1 red bell pepper, seeded and julienned
2 green onions, chopped
4 cloves garlic, minced
2 lemons, juiced
1 tsp salt
4 tbsp ghee

Directions

1. Drop ghee into skillet over medium heat.
2. Add all ingredients but shrimp, sauté for 5 minutes.
3. Add shrimp, cover for 2 minutes.
4. Serve.

Nutrition (g)

Calories 263
Fat 15
Sodium 861 (mg)
Carbs 5
Sugar 1
Protein 27

Shrimp and Mushroom Stir-Fry

Serves: 4
Preparation time: 5 minutes
Cooking Time: 7 minutes

Ingredients
1 ½ lb jumbo shrimp, peeled and deveined
6 cups button mushrooms, sliced
2 green onions, chopped
4 cloves garlic, minced
½ tsp salt
½ tsp black pepper
Olive oil
2 lemons

Directions

1. Heat 4 tbsp olive oil in skillet.
2. Add ingredients, stir-fry until shrimp is pink.
3. Squeeze a little lemon on top when serving.

Nutrition (g)
Calories 220
Fat 7
Sodium 573 (mg)
Carbs 8
Sugar 6
Protein 34

Fruity Nutty Tuna Salad

Serves: 4
Preparation time: 5 minutes
Cooking Time: 0 minutes

Ingredients
12 oz cooked tuna
4 cups romaine lettuce, chopped
¼ cup pecans
¼ cup dried fruits (cranberry, apricot)
¾ cup parsley, chopped
Balsamic Vinaigrette
5 tbsp balsamic vinegar
¼ cup extra virgin olive oil
½ tsp salt
½ tsp black pepper

Directions

1. Combine ingredients for vinaigrette in bowl, mix.
2. Place salad ingredients in bowl, toss with vinaigrette.

Nutrition (g)
Calories 263
Fat 15
Sodium 861 (mg)
Carbs 5
Sugar 1
Protein 27

Louisiana Crab Boil

Serves: 4
Preparation time: 5 minutes
Cooking Time: 20 minutes, 30 seconds

Ingredients

4 small Dungeness crabs
2 lbs shrimp, shelled and deveined
1 bulb fennel, chopped
8 cups water
2 tbsp ginger, grated
2 medium onions, chopped
2 celery stalks, chopped
2 lemons, juiced
4 cloves
4 peppercorns
1 tsp red pepper flakes
2 bay leaves.
3 tbsp sea salt

Directions

1. Combine ingredients except for

   shrimp and crab in a large soup pot and place on burner on high heat.

2. Bring to boil and boil for 10 minutes.
3. Add crab and continue boiling for 10 minutes.
4. Add shrimp and boil for 30 seconds.
5. Cover and remove from heat, allow to sit for 10 minutes before serving.

Nutrition (g)

Calories 529
Fat 8
Sodium 656 (mg)
Carbs 18
Sugar 3

Raspberry Smoked Salmon and Eggs

Serves: 4
Preparation time: 5 minutes
Cooking Time: 3 hours

Ingredients
½ lb smoked salmon
4 eggs
1 tsp dill
⅓ cup raspberries
1 tsp salt
Olive oil

Directions

1. Coat slow cooker with olive oil.
2. Place smoked salmon on bottom of slow cooker.
3. Top with raspberries, dill.
4. Crack eggs one by one.
5. Sprinkle with salt.
6. Cook on high for 3 hours.

Nutrition (g)
Calories 165
Fat 10
Sodium 1778 (mg)
Carbs 2
Sugar 1
Protein 16

VEGETARIAN RECIPES

Mediterranean Spinach, Walnut and Feta

Serves: 2
Preparation time: 5 minutes
Cooking Time: 3 hours

Ingredients

8 cups fresh spinach
1 medium onion, chopped
4 cloves garlic, minced
¼ cup walnuts, chopped
4 dates, pitted and chopped
½ cup feta cheese
1 tsp salt
1 tsp black pepper
Olive oil

Directions

1. Coat slow cooker with olive oil.
2. Layer spinach on bottom and top with remaining ingredients.
3. Cook on high for 3 hours.

Nutrition (g)

Calories 152
Fat 9
Sodium 840 (mg)
Carbs 14
Sugar 8
Protein 7

Slow-Cooked Green Eggs

Serves: 2
Preparation time: 5 minutes
Cooking Time:

Ingredients

6 cups kale, chopped
4 eggs
1 onion, chopped
1 tsp salt
1 tsp black pepper
ghee

Directions

1. Coat bottom of slow cooker with ghee.
2. Place kale and onion in bottom of slow cooker.
3. Crack one egg at a time on kale and onion.
4. Cook on low for 6 hours.

Nutrition (g)

Calories 181
Fat 11
Sodium 688 (mg)
Carbs 14
Sugar 1
Protein 9

Cranberry Avocado Spinach Salad

Serves: 2
Preparation time: 5 minutes
Cooking Time: 0 minutes

Ingredients

1 avocado, pitted and peeled
¼ cup walnuts chopped
¼ cup dried cranberries
4 cups baby spinach
2 tbsp balsamic vinegar
1 tsp salt
3 tbsp olive oil

Directions

1. Slice avocado into ½" cubes.
2. Combine olive oil, vinegar, and salt, and whisk.
3. Combine all ingredients in bowl, toss and serve.

Nutrition (g)

Calories 181
Fat 11
Sodium 688 (mg)
Carbs 14
Sugar 2
Protein 9

Cheesy Butternut Squash

Serves: 4
Preparation Time: 5 minutes.
Cooking Time: 45 minutes

Ingredients
1 butternut squash
¾ cup mozzarella cheese
1 tsp salt
coconut oil

Directions

1. Preheat oven to 400°F/204°C and coat a casserole dish with coconut oil.
2. Slice squash in half, scoop out seeds and fibres.
3. Set squash in casserole dish, brush flesh with coconut oil, sprinkle with salt and cheese.
4. Cover dish with aluminum foil and bake in oven for 45 minutes.

Nutrition (g)
Calories 134
Fat 11
Sodium 710 (mg)
Carbs 5
Sugar 1
Protein 6

Cauliflower Coconut Curry

Serves: 2
Preparation time: 5 minutes
Cooking Time: 7 hours

Ingredients
1 medium head cauliflower, divided into florets
2 carrots, chopped
1 medium onion, chopped
1 red bell pepper, seeded, chopped
2 tbsp tomato paste
1 can coconut milk
4 cups low-sodium chicken stock
1 tsp curry powder
1 tsp salt
1 tsp black pepper

Directions

1. Place ingredients in slow cooker and cook on low for 7 hours.

Nutrition (g)
Calories 221
Fat 15
Sodium 800 (mg)
Carbs 20
Sugar 10
Protein 7

Cheesy Stuffed Frittata

Serves: 2
Preparation time: 10 minutes
Cooking Time: 3 hours

Ingredients

6 eggs
1 cup broccoli florets, chopped
1 tomato, diced
1 green onion, diced
2 tbsp milk
1 tbsp almond flour
½ cup cheddar cheese, grated.
½ tsp salt
½ tsp black pepper
Olive oil

Directions

1. Whisk eggs with remaining ingredients.
2. Coat slow cooker with olive oil.
3. Pour egg mixture into slow cooker.
4. Cook on high for 3 hours.

Nutrition (g)

Calories 415
Fat 30
Sodium 972 (mg)
Carbs 9
Sugar 4
Protein 29

Squash Soup

Serves: 4
Preparation time: 10 minutes
Cooking Time: 8 hours

Ingredients

4 summer squash, peeled, chopped
1 can coconut milk
4 cups low-sodium chicken stock
1 tsp salt
1 tsp black pepper

Directions

1. Place ingredients in slow cooker, mix.
2. Cook on low for 8 hours.
3. Once cooked, use a hand immersion blender and mix until smooth.

Nutrition (g)

Calories 162
Fat 15
Sodium 728 (mg)
Carbs 7
Sugar 5
Protein 3

Arugula Salad

Serves: 4
Preparation time: 5 minutes
Cooking Time: 0 minutes

Ingredients
6 cups arugula, chopped
1 cup cherry tomatoes, halved
1 red onion, sliced
1 tbsp flaxseed
½ cup walnuts, chopped
Balsamic Vinaigrette
5 tbsp balsamic vinegar
¼ cup extra virgin olive oil
½ tsp salt

Directions

1. Mix vinegar and salt in bowl, slowly add olive oil while whisking.
2. Place ingredients for salad in large bowl, add vinaigrette and toss.

Nutrition (g)
Calories 244
Fat 23
Sodium 304 (mg)
Carbs 7
Sugar 3
Protein 6

Tofu Scramble

Serves: 2
Preparation time: 5 minutes
Cooking Time: 7 minutes

Ingredients
1 small pkg firm tofu
1 small onion, chopped
1 green bell pepper, seeded, chopped
3 tbsp ghee
½ tsp salt
½ tsp black pepper

Directions

1. Heat ghee in skillet over medium.
2. Add remaining ingredients and scramble.
3. Scramble until moisture evaporates and tofu reaches egg-like consistency.

Nutrition (g)
Calories 290
Fat 25
Sodium 601 (mg)
Carbs 9
Sugar 5
Protein 11

Parmesan and Green Bean Bake

Serves: 4
Preparation time: 5 minutes
Cooking Time: 35 minutes

Ingredients

6 cups fresh green beans
¼ cup Parmesan, shredded
¼ cup coconut milk
½ tsp salt
½ tsp black pepper
Coconut oil

Directions

1. Preheat oven to 400°F/204°C, lightly coat a casserole dish with olive oil.
2. Dump beans, coconut milk, salt, and black pepper in dish, cover with aluminium foil and bake in oven for 35 minutes.

Nutrition (g)

Calories 208
Fat 14
Sodium 438 (mg)
Carbs 17
Sugar 4
Protein 9

Conclusion

Eating low-carb can be simple, easy, and delicious. All you need is a cooking vessel and this book and you're well on your way to a clean, simple, slim life.

Low-carb eating can mean different things to different people. For some, low-carb eating means a free-for-all cheese and bacon fest, while for others it means more natural foods without the chemicals and potential harmful effects of processing.

In order to stick to a low-carb plan you need to find the best mix for you, if adding a little bacon to your dishes when you begin is going to help you stay away from the bread than by all means add a little. But the best thing to do is progress toward clean, natural eating that your body is easily able to process.

Appendix – Cooking Conversion Charts

1. Measuring Equivalent Chart

Type	Imperial	Imperial	Metric
Weight	1 dry ounce		28g
	1 pound	16 dry ounces	0.45 kg
Volume	1 teaspoon		5 ml
	1 dessert spoon	2 teaspoons	10 ml
	1 tablespoon	3 teaspoons	15 ml
	1 Australian tablespoon	4 teaspoons	20 ml
	1 fluid ounce	2 tablespoons	30 ml
	1 cup	16 tablespoons	240 ml
	1 cup	8 fluid ounces	240 ml
	1 pint	2 cups	470 ml
	1 quart	2 pints	0.95 l
	1 gallon	4 quarts	3.8 l
Length	1 inch		2.54 cm

* Numbers are rounded to the closest equivalent

2. Oven Temperature Equivalent Chart

Fahrenheit (°F)	Celsius (°C)	Gas Mark
220	100	
225	110	1/4
250	120	1/2
275	140	1
300	150	2
325	160	3
350	180	4
375	190	5
400	200	6
425	220	7
450	230	8
475	250	9
500	260	

* Celsius (°C) = T (°F)-32] * 5/9
** Fahrenheit (°F) = T (°C) * 9/5 + 32
*** Numbers are rounded to the closest equivalent